Crossing
the
DELAWARE

For Elliott—L.P.
For the Roucloux Family—W.L.K.

EDITOR'S NOTE: THIS BOOK CONTAINS BOTH FICTION AND NONFICTION. ALL EXCERPTS FROM ACTUAL LETTERS AND DIARIES ARE ACCOMPANIED BY CREDITS INDICATING THEIR AUTHORS. THE LETTERS OF HARRY, THE SOLDIER THE READER FOLLOWS THROUGHOUT, ARE FICTION.

ISBN 0-439-13309-2

12 11 10 9 8 7 6 5 4 3 2 1   9/9 0 1 2 3 4/0

PRINTED IN THE U.S.A.   14

FIRST SCHOLASTIC PRINTING, OCTOBER 1999

WASHINGTON AND THE BATTLE OF TRENTON, ENGRAVING BY ILLMAN BROTHERS FROM A PAINTING BY E.L. HENRY, COURTESY OF THE NATIONAL ARCHIVES.
COVER ILLUSTRATION COPYRIGHT © 1998 BY WALTER LYON KRUDOP

SPECIAL THANKS TO VINCE ROSPOND FOR HIS ASSISTANCE
BOOK DESIGN BY PATTI RATCHFORD
THE TEXT OF THIS BOOK IS SET IN ADOBE CASLON

ART CREDITS: FRONT ENDPAPERS: (BOSTON MASSACRE) CHROMOLITHOGRAPH BY JOHN BUFFORD; (BOSTON TEA PARTY) LITHOGRAPH BY SARONY AND MAJOR; (PAUL REVERE'S RIDE) UNKNOWN; (BATTLE OF LEXINGTON) DRAWING FROM ENGRAVING BY AMOS DOOLITTLE; (RETREAT FROM CONCORD) UNKNOWN; (CAPTURE OF FORT TICONDEROGA) ENGRAVING FROM PAINTING BY ALONZO CHAPPEL; (BATTLE OF BUNKER HILL) ENGRAVING FROM PAINTING BY JOHN TRUMBULL; (BATTLE OF BUNKER HILL AND THE BURNING OF CHARLESTOWN) ENGRAVING BY LODGE FROM DRAWING BY MILLAR; (WASHINGTON TAKES COMMAND AT CAMBRIDGE) ENGRAVING BY C. ROGERS FROM PAINTING BY M. A. WAGEMAN; (2ND CONTINENTAL CONGRESS) PAINTING BY ROBERT PINE AND EDWARD SAVAGE; (READING OF THE DECLARATION OF INDEPENDENCE, BOSTON) UNKNOWN. **INTERIOR:** WATERCOLOR BY THOMAS DAVIES, 5; ENGRAVING FROM PAINTING BY ALONZO CHAPPEL, 8; ENGRAVING BY J. C. ARMYTAGE FROM PAINTING BY M. A. WAGEMAN, 9; PAINTING BY GILBERT STUART, 10; ENGRAVING BY J. WARD FROM PAINTING BY SIR W. BEECHEY, 15; CARTOON IN LINE ENGRAVING BY PAUL REVERE, 17; PAINTING BY EMANUEL LEUTZE, 28; ENGRAVING BY ILLMAN BROTHERS FROM PAINTING BY E. L. HENRY, 32; LITHOGRAPH BY HENRY HOFF, 34; ENGRAVING BY HOLL FROM PAINTING BY FAED, 36; PAINTING BY A. M. WILLARD, 40. **BACK ENDPAPERS:** (BATTLE OF PRINCETON) LITHOGRAPH BY D. MCLELLAN; (BATTLE OF GERMANTOWN) ENGRAVING BY RAWDON, WRIGHT, AND HARCH FROM DRAWING BY KOELTNER; (BURGOYNE'S SURRENDER) PAINTING BY JOHN TRUMBULL; (BARON VON STEUBEN AT VALLEY FORGE) PAINTING BY AUGUSTUS G. HEATON; (MOLLY PITCHER AT THE BATTLE OF MONMOUTH) ENGRAVING BY J. C. ARMYTAGE FROM PAINTING BY ALONZO CHAPPEL; (BATTLE BETWEEN HMS SERAPIS AND THE BONHOMME RICHARD) ENGRAVING FROM PAINTING BY RICHARD PATON; (CLARK'S MARCH TO VINCENNES) PAINTING BY EZRA WINTER; (BATTLE OF CAMDEN) ENGRAVING FROM PAINTING BY ALONZO CHAPPEL; (CORNWALLIS'S SURRENDER) PAINTING BY JOHN TRUMBULL; (WASHINGTON ENTERS NEW YORK CITY) ENGRAVING BY A. H. RITCHIE; (WASHINGTON'S FAREWELL TO HIS OFFICERS) ENGRAVING BY PHILLIBROWN FROM PAINTING BY ALONZO CHAPPEL.

Crossing

the

DELAWARE

A HISTORY IN MANY VOICES

by Louise Peacock

ILLUSTRATED BY WALTER LYON KRUDOP

SCHOLASTIC INC.

New York   Toronto   London   Auckland   Sydney
Mexico City   New Delhi   Hong Kong

THE HOUSE OF DECISIONS IS VERY OLD. IT WAS OLD IN DECEMBER OF 1776, WHEN THE MERRICK FAMILY LOANED IT TO GENERAL WASHINGTON, WHEN THE REVOLUTIONARY WAR WAS JUST BEGINNING. IT WAS OLD WHEN GENERAL WASHINGTON MET HIS OFFICERS HERE, WHEN HE MADE HIS DESPERATE DECISION.

THE FARMHOUSE STANDS ALONE ON THE BANK OF THE DELAWARE RIVER. WHEN I GO INTO THE HOUSE, I REST MY HAND ON THE STONE WALL. GENERAL WASHINGTON WOULD HAVE TOUCHED THIS WALL TOO, WHEN HE WENT INTO THE HOUSE AND WHEN HE CAME OUT.

December 8

Dearest Jenny,

We crossed the river safely into Pennsylvania today, and are encamped right along the bank. It's very cold here. The Captain has managed to get us quartered in a shed, so we are warmer than most. Tom even found a bit of straw in the mow, so we'll rest in comfort tonight. The Fifteenth came across this evening, and they're sleeping in the open, so you know how fortunate we are to be under a roof.

We have sentries posted up and down the bank, looking for Redcoat movement across the river in Jersey. We all figure they'll try to follow us across the Delaware if they can. Don't worry—they can't sneak up on us!

Harry

British forces landing in the Jerseys, Nov. 20, 1776

This was the crisis of American danger. We lay amongst the leaves without tents or blankets, laying down with our feet to the fire. It was very cold.

Captain Enoch Anderson
Personal Recollections

WHEN GENERAL WASHINGTON STAYED IN THIS HOUSE, THE ENGLISH ARMY WAS JUST ACROSS THE RIVER IN TRENTON. THEY WERE A STRONG FIGHTING FORCE. THEY WERE HESSIANS, PROFESSIONAL SOLDIERS FROM GERMANY, THE BEST TRAINED TROOPS KING GEORGE COULD HIRE. THE SOLDIERS IN THE CONTINENTAL ARMY WERE FARMERS AND MERCHANTS AND SMITHS, UNTRAINED VOLUNTEERS FROM ALL THIRTEEN COLONIES WHO HAD LEARNED WHAT THEY KNEW ABOUT WARFARE ONLY FROM THE BATTLES THEY'D FOUGHT.

THEY WERE COLD AND HUNGRY AND SICK AND TIRED. THEY SLEPT IN THE SNOW, WRAPPED IN THEIR BLANKETS. THEY WERE DRESSED IN RAGS, AND SOMETIMES THEIR FEET LEFT BLOODY FOOTPRINTS IN THE SNOW.

December 9

Dear Jenny,

We've been up and down the banks of the river today, making sure all the boats on our side are under strong guard and none are left on the Jersey shore at all. I do not think the British can hope for a crossing until the river freezes to thick ice.

I'm wearing that second set of stockings you made me, Jenny. Believe me, I'm mighty glad to have 'em! Plenty of fellows have worn their boots through and have to make do with rags wrapped around their feet, but thanks to you I'm in fine shape. My feet don't ever touch the snow.

Suddenly a man staggered out of the line and came toward me. He had lost all his clothes.
He was in an old dirty blanket-jacket, his beard long and his face full
of sores . . . which so disfigured him that he was not known by me on first sight. Only
when he spoke did I recognize my brother James.

Charles Willson Peale
journal

Battle of Long Island

WORST OF ALL, THE SOLDIERS WERE DISCOURAGED. THE ARMY HAD NOT WON A SINGLE BATTLE. THEY HAD LOST LONG ISLAND IN AUGUST, NEW YORK IN SEPTEMBER, AND WHITE PLAINS IN OCTOBER, AND ALWAYS THEY'D KEPT RETREATING, MOVING SOUTH ONE JUMP AHEAD OF THE BRITISH. THEY'D CROSSED RIVER AFTER RIVER—PASSAIC, RAHWAY, RARITAN, MILLSTONE, AND FINALLY THE DELAWARE.

THE SOLDIERS WERE ALL AFRAID THE REVOLUTION MIGHT BE OVER. THERE WAS ONLY THE ARMY LEFT, AND MANY PEOPLE SAID THEY WERE FOOLISH TO FIGHT.

THE SOLDIERS HAD ONLY PROMISED TO FIGHT FOR SIX MONTHS WHEN THEY JOINED THE ARMY IN THE SPRING. IT HAD BEEN A HARD TIME. THEY HAD LOST BATTLES. THEY HAD LOST FRIENDS. SOME OF THEM HAD EVEN LOST THEIR DREAM OF FREEDOM. MOST OF THEM WOULD BE FREE TO GO HOME IN JUST A FEW DAYS, ON JANUARY FIRST. THE ARMY WOULD BE GONE. THE REVOLUTION WOULD BE OVER.

*I have to say I'm mighty sick of this war. I still believe in our
Cause, Jenny—I always will—but we've done nothing but retreat.
We're not cowards if we come home now, nor traitors neither. What's
the point of fighting if you never win? Maybe Pa was right, and this
was all foolishness. Most of the fellows say they will be going home on
January 1st, when our enlistments are up. I guess I will be coming
with them. It'll be fine to see you again. Say hello to your brother
John for me, and tell him I can help with the planting this spring.*

Harry

Retreat at Long Island

You may as well attempt to stop the Winds from blowing, or the Sun in its diurnal, as the
Regiments from going when their term is expired.

Washington to Robert Morris

Something must be attempted before the sixty days expire . . . I will not disguise my
own sentiments, that our cause is desperate and hopeless if we do not take the
opportunity of the collection of troops at present, to strike some stroke. Our affairs are
hastening fast to ruin if we do not retrieve them by some happy event.
Delay with us is equal to total defeat.

Colonel Joseph Reed to General Washington

General George Washington

I STAND BESIDE THE GENERAL'S DESK, WHERE HE WROTE HIS LETTERS, AND TRY TO IMAGINE IT. NO REVOLUTIONARY WAR. NO UNITED STATES OF AMERICA. WHERE WOULD I BE LIVING NOW IF THE GENERAL HAD FAILED? WHAT WOULD MY LIFE BE LIKE?

Past experience has repeatedly convinced us, that Troops, at the most favorable Season of the year and well supplied with every Necessary, cannot be prevailed upon to stay a day longer than what they engaged for; . . . it cannot be expected, that Men worn out with a fatiguing Campaign and in want of even necessary Cloathing, at the most inclement Season of the Year, will or can stay beyond their Engagement. . . . When I reflect, upon what our Situation in this Quarter will be, in ten days from this time; I am almost led to despair.

Washington to Governor Jonathan Trumbull

THAT DECEMBER, THERE WERE THREE FULL HESSIAN REGIMENTS IN TRENTON, AND THERE WERE MANY MORE BRITISH TROOPS IN TOWNS NEARBY. THE BRITISH TROOPS WERE WELL FED AND RESTED AND WARM. THE 2400 AMERICAN SOLDIERS STILL STRONG AND HEALTHY ENOUGH TO FIGHT WERE HUNGRY AND COLD AND TIRED AND DISCOURAGED. WHAT COULD GENERAL WASHINGTON DO?

HE DECIDED TO ATTACK.

IT WAS SUCH A DESPERATE THING TO DO.

December 16

Dear Jenny,

We're keeping a sharp watch on the river, as you can imagine. Everyone thinks Howe still plans to winter in Philadelphia. I can't help but wonder what will become of the folk there if he does. They must be mighty fine people. They took up a collection of old clothes for us, and I have a second shirt to wear now. With that and your socks, I'm warmer than any man here!

Tom had a bit of luck today. The Captain sent us out foraging, and at the second farmhouse we stopped, Tom saw a pair of boots sitting next to the fireplace. The farmer didn't want to sell them, but when Tom showed his wife the state his feet were in, she said he could buy 'em.

You never saw a fellow so happy! He says he can walk like a regular man again. We've put more grease on the cracks in his feet, and we figure they'll heal pretty soon.

I'm mighty glad he has those boots. It's going to be a long walk home. I hope our last pay comes through all right, so we'll be able to eat good on the way.

Harry

I have no doubt but that General Howe will still make an attempt upon Philadelphia this Winter. I see nothing to oppose him a fortnight hence, as the time of all the Troops . . . will expire in less than that time. In a word my dear Sir, *if every nerve is not strain'd to* recruit the New Army with all possible expedition, *I think the game is pretty near up.* . . . You can form no Idea of the perplexity of my Situation. No Man, I believe, ever had a greater choice of difficulties and less means to extricate himself from them.

Washington to John Augustine Washington

GENERAL WASHINGTON KNEW THAT AT HOME THE HESSIANS ALWAYS CELEBRATED CHRISTMAS WITH A BIG PARTY. THEY WOULD PROBABLY DO THE SAME THING IN AMERICA. IF THE GENERAL AND HIS MEN CROSSED THE RIVER CHRISTMAS DAY, WHILE THE PARTY WAS GOING ON, THERE WAS A CHANCE THEY COULD SURPRISE THE HESSIANS. THERE WAS JUST A SMALL CHANCE THEY COULD WIN THE VICTORY THE AMERICANS NEEDED.

IT WAS A DESPERATE THING TO DO.

December 20

Dear Jenny,

I saw the General himself today! He came past as we mustered. He looked very grave, I thought, but not in the least downcast. It makes me wonder if he has some plan.

The fellows are saying old Cornwallis is sailing back to England to tell King George we're licked. Makes me mad just to think about that!

Lord Charles Cornwallis

A scout . . . says that Howe and Cornwallis are well satisfied with what they have accomplished. Cornwallis is going to England to tell the King that the rebellion is about over. Howe is going to have a good time in New York attending dinner parties. From what I see I am quite certain Washington intends to make some movement soon.

He keeps his own counsel, but is very much determined.

Officer on Washington's staff

diary

ON THE EVENING OF DECEMBER 24TH WASHINGTON HELD HIS COUNCIL OF WAR HERE, IN THIS OLD STONE FARMHOUSE. I STAND IN THE DOORWAY AND IMAGINE THAT MEETING.

THE ARMY WAS DIVIDED INTO THREE GROUPS. THEY WOULD ALL CROSS THE RIVER ON CHRISTMAS NIGHT—ONE GROUP AT BORDENTOWN, ONE AT TRENTON FERRY, AND THE MAIN ARMY WITH WASHINGTON AT MCKONKEY'S FERRY JUST DOWN THE ROAD. THEY WOULD CROSS BACK INTO NEW JERSEY AND ATTACK TRENTON FROM DIFFERENT DIRECTIONS. THEY PLANNED TO MARCH THROUGH THE NIGHT AND ATTACK BEFORE DAWN ON THE 26TH.

COLONEL RALL, THE HESSIAN COMMANDER IN TRENTON, DESPISED THE AMERICANS. HE WAS NOT EXPECTING ANY ATTACK. HE WOULD BE VERY SURPRISED TO SEE GENERAL WASHINGTON AND HIS TROOPS. PERHAPS THAT SURPRISE WOULD HELP WIN THE BATTLE.

IT WAS A DESPERATE THING TO DO.

The thing is, they think we're good for nothing. Old King George thinks he can do anything to us, and we'll just swallow it and do what we're told. But it's not right, Jenny. It's just not right. Pa says there's naught to be done about it. I can't believe that. We are free men and women here, and we have to keep our liberty. Those Hessian troops are mighty tough, though. They despise us. They think we can't do anything.

[They are] nothing but a lot of farmers . . . If they come, all they can hope for is a good retreat.

Colonel Rall, commander of Hessian troops in Trenton

"The able doctor, or America swallowing the bitter draught," cartoon in line engraving by Paul Revere

I LEAVE THE HOUSE OF DECISIONS AND WALK DOWN THE ROAD TOWARD THE FORD, WHERE MCKONKEY'S FERRY USED TO BE. I IMAGINE GENERAL WASHINGTON WALKING TALL BESIDE ME. PERHAPS HE HAD A PATCH ON HIS BOOT AS HE STEPPED THROUGH THE SNOW. PERHAPS HIS HANDS WERE COLD IN THE WINTER NIGHT.

I WONDER WHAT HE THOUGHT AS HE WALKED DOWN TO THE RIVER. I WONDER WHAT THOSE RAGGED MEN WHO FOLLOWED HIM THOUGHT. WERE THEY FRIGHTENED? OR WERE THEY DETERMINED?

WOULD THEY GO HOME IN EIGHT DAYS, ON THE FIRST OF JANUARY, AND CALL THE REVOLUTION OVER?

I'd keep fighting if I saw any hope in it. Everyone here would. It isn't the cold that's licked us, or hunger either, and we know we're doing right. But we never win, Jenny. Every battle's been a defeat, and every move's been a retreat. It takes the heart out of a man.

The Captain is trying to get us all to renew our enlistments, but nobody has signed up again, not even me. I think it's the same in every brigade. Most fellows just want to go back home and forget about it. There's not much left to hope for.

Harry

The time of enlistment of Ewing's brigade . . . all expire the first of Jan. next and . . . the officers and men and Gen. Ewing himself have declared that they will serve no longer . . . [Of] the New England troops who came with General Washington it is generally believed from their declaration that they will not serve longer than the term of their enlistment, which expires also the First of Jan'y next . . .

Samuel Brown, informer to the British

AT THE FORD I STAND BESIDE A DURHAM BOAT. IT'S ABOUT THIRTY FEET LONG, LONGER THAN OUR CAR, AND IT'S PAINTED BLACK. THIS IS THE KIND OF BOAT THE AMERICANS USED TO CROSS THE DELAWARE RIVER THAT NIGHT.

HOW DID THEY FIND THE COURAGE TO DO IT?

IT WAS SUCH A DESPERATE THING TO DO.

We looked upon the contest as near its close, and considered ourselves a vanquished people. . . . Major Thomas animated our desponding spirits by the assurance that Washington was not dismayed, but evinced the same serenity and confidence as ever. Upon him rested all our hopes.

Elkanah Watson
Memoirs

I have waited with much Impatience to know the determinations of Congress
on the Propositions made . . . for augmenting our Corps . . . It may be thought that, I am
going a good deal out of the line of my duty to adopt these Measures, or advise
thus freely; A Character to loose, an Estate to forfeit, the inestimable Blessing of liberty
at Stake, and a life devoted, must be my excuse.

Washington to the President of Congress

I LOOK ACROSS THE RIVER TO THE NEW JERSEY SHORE. I CAN SEE THE SHORELINE, BUT IT IS A LONG WAY AWAY. HUGE CHUNKS OF ICE RUSH PAST, SWIRLING IN THE RIVER'S CURRENT.

I THINK OF THOSE COLD, HUNGRY MEN ROWING THESE SMALL BOATS ACROSS THE RIVER IN DARKNESS, WILLING TO FIGHT ONE MORE TIME FOR THEIR DREAM.

December 23

Dear Jenny,

We were out checking for boats again today. The Captain said to make sure every available craft was drawn up near McKonkey's Ferry. It makes me wonder what's being planned. If Washington didn't have some plan, we could just burn the boats so the Redcoats couldn't cross. I think he must have something in mind.

The General had Mr. Paine's proclamation read out to us at muster. He's been marching with the Army all summer, you know. Have you seen a copy at home yet? Read it out loud to the little ones, Jenny. It made me stand taller just to hear the words, and I could see everybody else felt the same way about it. We're no summer soldiers, Jenny, nor sunshine patriots neither, and we're not licked quite yet. I reckon we've got one more good shout left in us anyway.

The orders are to keep three days' rations cooked and ready. Something must be going to happen soon.

Harry

These are the times that try men's souls. The summer soldier and sunshine patriot will, in this crisis, shrink from the service of their country; but he that stands it now deserves the love and thanks of man and woman. Tyranny, like hell, is not easily conquered; yet we have this consolation with us, that the harder the conflict, the more glorious the triumph . . . Up and help us; lay your shoulder to the wheel; the heart that feels not now, is dead.

Thomas Paine
"The American Crisis"

I **TRY TO IMAGINE** WHAT IT WOULD BE LIKE TO BE THAT BRAVE. COULD I MARCH BAREFOOT IN THE SNOW? COULD I CROSS AN ICE-FILLED RIVER IN THE DARK?

Christmas, 6 p.m.— It is fearfully cold and raw and a snow-storm [is] setting in. The wind is northeast and beats in the faces of the men. It will be a terrible night for the soldiers who have no shoes. Some of them have tied old rags around their feet; others are barefoot, but I have not heard a man complain. They are ready to suffer any hardship and die rather than give up their liberty. I have just copied the order for marching.

Officer on Washington's staff
diary

Christmas

Dear Jenny,

I'm writing from the tavern at the ferry. The Captain sent me in with a message so I'm taking the chance to warm myself at the fire. We're on the move, Jenny!

When we turned out for muster today we didn't go back to quarters, but kept marching on down the bank. The dark is drawing in fast, and the wind is awful cold. The Captain and all the other officers have put bits of white paper in their hats, so we can make them out even in the gloom.

It's the men from Marblehead handling the boats. They're a wonder, Jenny! I don't know how they get 'em across, with the current running so fast and those big chunks of ice carried along. It's taking a long time to load and cross, and it's a mighty cold wait here. There's snow settling in. I'm mighty glad of those extra socks tonight, Jenny. I'm thinking of the way you look, with your head bent over the knitting needles and the firelight shining on your hair. I'll write another line soon as I get the chance.

Crossing the Delaware

GENERAL WASHINGTON WAS ONE OF THE FIRST MEN ON THE NEW JERSEY SHORE. HIS OFFICERS THOUGHT HE SHOULD GO INSIDE AND STAND BY A WARM FIRE. HE REFUSED. HE FOUND AN OLD EMPTY BEE-HIVE AND SAT ON IT ALL NIGHT, THE SNOW AND THE SLEET BEATING DOWN ON HIM, WATCHING HIS ARMY CROSS THE RIVER.

Dec. 26, 3 a.m.— I never have seen Washington so determined as he is now. He stands on the bank of the river, wrapped in his cloak, superintending the landing of his troops. He is calm and collected, but very determined. The storm is changing to sleet, and cuts like a knife. . . . We are ready to mount our horses.

Officer on Washington's staff
diary

We're back on the Jersey side of the river now, Jenny, and partway to Trenton. There's a crossroad here, and we've stopped for a bit.

The General himself stood on the bank to watch us as we came ashore. I saluted him when our boys marched past and I'll swear he nodded to me. It's very dark, and the sleet is cutting, but he's been there all night. We're all taking our lead from him, and setting off quiet and determined toward Trenton. We'll show them a thing or two come morning, Jenny.

EVERYONE TRIED TO BE AS QUIET AS POSSIBLE. THE MEN WHIS-
PERED THE PASSWORD OF THE DAY WHEN THEY MET IN THE DARKNESS:
"VICTORY OR DEATH."

I WONDER HOW THEY FELT WHEN THEY MARCHED DOWN THAT ROAD
THROUGH THE DARKNESS, CARRYING GUNS THAT MIGHT NOT EVEN
SHOOT. THEIR FACES WERE LASHED BY THE WIND AND THE SLEET. THEIR
FEET WERE BLEEDING. WERE THEY FRIGHTENED? DID THEY WANT TO
TURN BACK?

IT WAS SUCH A DESPERATE THING TO DO.

*We've got a boy marching with us now who fell behind his troop. I
think the cold must have numbed him, for he was leaning against a tree
when Tom spotted him and could hardly move. We've made him get up
and walk along, and we're keeping him between us so he can't sit down
again. A fellow could freeze on the side of the road on a night like this.*

*I've spoken to Tom, and he promises to bring this letter to you if
anything should happen to me in the morning.*

Harry

As we had been in the storm all night we were not only wet through and through
ourselves, but our guns and powder were wet also, so that I do not believe that one would
go off, and I saw none fired by our party. When we were all ready we advanced and,
although there was not more than one bayonet to five men, orders were given to 'Charge
bayonets and rush on!' and rush on we did.

Private Greenwood, age 16

Washington at the Battle of Trenton

GENERAL WASHINGTON'S TROOPS REACHED TRENTON ABOUT AN HOUR AFTER SUNRISE, BUT THE HESSIANS WERE STILL SURPRISED. AT FIRST, THEY COULD HARDLY BELIEVE THEY WERE BEING ATTACKED. COLONEL RALL DID NOT GET OUT OF BED UNTIL HIS MEN HAD REPORTED ENEMY FIRE TWICE. THE SOUNDS OF GUNFIRE AND THE GUARDS' SHOUTS OF *"DER FEIND! HERAUS!"* "THE ENEMY! TURN OUT!" RANG THROUGH THE TOWN.

RALL WAS TOO LATE TO GET HIS MEN INTO BATTLE FORMATION, AND THE AMERICANS PUSHED THE HESSIAN SOLDIERS BACK THROUGH TOWN. HOW EXCITED THE AMERICANS MUST HAVE BEEN!

December 27

Jenny, love,

You've never seen such a fight! It was full dawn when we reached Trenton, but the Enemy never even saw us. We rushed into the town with a shout, and everywhere they fell back before us.

Some of the citizens had managed to hide their muskets, and they came out to join us, so our forces grew bigger as we went through the town. I even saw one woman firing a musket from her window! The Hessians just ran before us. We've captured a passel of their men, and what the General will do with 'em I don't know. But not one of our fellows was killed!

There's never been a victory like this, Jenny, never! You should see the faces of the men. We're all singing and laughing and slapping each other on the back. We haven't felt like this since spring. It's victory, Jenny!

Harry

It is a glorious victory. It will rejoice the hearts of our friends everywhere and give new life to our hitherto waning fortunes. Washington has baffled the enemy . . . He has pounced upon the Hessians like an eagle upon a hen.

Officer on Washington's staff

Surrender of the Hessian troops after the Battle of Trenton

COLONEL RALL DIED IN THE BATTLE, AND THE AMERICANS CAPTURED THE TOWN. THEY CAPTURED 868 HESSIAN SOLDIERS, AND KILLED OR WOUNDED 106 MORE. THEY CAPTURED SIX CANNONS, ONE THOUSAND MUSKETS, AND A FULL SET OF BAND INSTRUMENTS! BEST OF ALL, NO AMERICANS WERE KILLED, AND ONLY FOUR WERE WOUNDED.

IT WAS A VICTORY!

I have the pleasure of Congratulating you upon the success of an enterprize which I had formed against a Detachment of the Enemy lying in Trenton, and which was executed yesterday Morning. . . . In justice to the Officers and Men, I must add, that their Behaviour upon this Occasion, reflects the highest honor upon them. The difficulty of passing the River in a very severe Night, and their march thro' a violent Storm of Snow and Hail, did not in the least abate their Ardour. But when they came to the Charge, each seemed to vie with the other in pressing forward . . .

Washington to the President of Congress

Washington Receiving a Salute on the Field of Trenton

BUT FOR ALL THE JUBILATION, MANY SOLDIERS PREPARED TO GO HOME AFTER THE BATTLE. THEY WERE STILL HUNGRY AND COLD, SICK AND TIRED. THEIR TERM OF ENLISTMENT WOULD BE OVER ON JANUARY FIRST. NOT EVEN THE OFFER OF A TEN DOLLAR BOUNTY COULD CONVINCE THEM TO STAY.

IN THE LAST DAYS OF DECEMBER, THE TROOPS WERE PARADED. THE OFFICERS MADE SPEECH AFTER SPEECH, ASKING THE SOLDIERS TO FIGHT JUST A LITTLE LONGER.

THOSE TIRED, RAGGED MEN STOOD IN FORMATION AND LISTENED TO THE OFFICERS SPEAK. THEY MUST HAVE THOUGHT ABOUT THE LONG SUMMER OF RETREAT, WHEN WASHINGTON'S MANEUVERS SAVED THE ARMY AND THE REVOLUTION. THEY MUST HAVE THOUGHT ABOUT CROSSING THE ICE-FILLED RIVER. I'M SURE THEY THOUGHT ABOUT THEIR VICTORY, AND ABOUT FREEDOM.

General Washington . . . ordered our regiment to be paraded, and personally addressed us, urging that we should stay a month longer. . . .

The General wheeled his horse about, rode in front of the regiment, and addressing us again, said, "My brave fellows, you have done all I have asked you to do, and more than could be reasonably expected. But your country is at stake, your wives, your houses and all that you hold dear. You have worn yourself out with fatigues and hardships, but we know not how to spare you. If you will consent to stay only one month longer, you will render that service to the cause of liberty and to your country which you probably never can do under any other circumstances. The present is emphatically the crisis which is to decide our destiny."

Sergeant R.

When the officers called them to reenlist, the soldiers stepped forward. Not just one or two, but hundreds, thousands. Some regiments gave three cheers.

The Army was staying.

I shiver when I think about that. After a summer of retreat, they had won a battle, and they stayed. The Revolution was not over at all. It had just begun.

December 30

Dearest Jenny,

The Rhode Islanders paraded today and General Mifflin addressed them, asking them to reenlist. He must have sounded mighty fine, because they've all agreed to stay. Colonel Stark has talked all his New Hampshire men into staying too, for another six weeks.

Tom and I have talked it over, and when General Washington asks us tomorrow, we'll be staying on a bit longer. Everybody here says the same.

I know this isn't what I told you before Trenton, Jenny. I hope you're not too disappointed. But it's what we have to do.

Last spring I told you we'd have a quick war, and be free before Christmas. Well, I see now that's not the way it's going to be. But we can win, Jenny. We've just proved it. If we can win a battle like this one, we can win our freedom too.

Love,
Harry

I have the pleasure to acquaint you that the Continental Regiments from the Eastern Governments, have, to a Man, agreed to stay Six weeks beyond their Term of Inlistment, which was to have expired the last day of this Month. . . .

Washington to the Officer commanding at Morristown

It is impossible to *beat* the notion of liberty out of these people. It is rooted in 'em from childhood.

General Thomas Gage

Spirit of '76